First published 1989 by Whitecap Books (Toronto) Ltd.
Suite 4O3—77 Mowat Avenue, Toronto, Ontario M6K 3E3

Book Design by Brad Nickason
Introduction by Michael Kluckner
Photo Editing by Brad Nickason
Edited by Elaine Jones

Canadian Cataloguing in Publication Data

Main entry under title:

Vancouver and the Lower Mainland

ISBN 0-921396-14-7

1. Vancouver (B.C.) - Description - Views.
2. Lower Mainland Region (B.C.) - Description and
travel - Views.
FC3847.37.V36 1989   971.13300222   C89-091115-0
F1089.5.V22V36 1989

Printed and bound in Canada by Friesen Printers.

Previous page: *Vancouver from Queen Elizabeth Park.*

Opposite: *The Sun Tower and B.C. Place Stadium.*

VANCOUVER
And The Lower Mainland

Introduction by Michael Kluckner

Contents

Introduction

Vancouver has recently shed its frontier, lumber-town image to emerge as a thriving international city in a spectacular natural setting. Tourists and recent arrivals thrill to the contrast between Vancouver and the rest of Canada: winter with a small "w," rose gardening at Christmas, skiing in the morning and windsurfing in the afternoon, easy commutes from not-so-distant suburbs, no need for air conditioning in the summertime, and optional snow tires for the family car. Vancouver is unusual among world cities, and unique in Canada, for its combination of the natural and the urban, the recreational and the cultural, the relative lack of pollution and the opportunities for business and industry.

Vancouver's splendid natural setting has an excellent combination of water, farmland, space for housing, land for parks and recreation, and access routes for transportation. The surprising thing is that, historically, the city of Vancouver is a relative latecomer to the southern coast of British Columbia. The site was, in fact, a stagnant, two-bit sawmill town of a few hundred people, utterly insignificant beside the old colonial capital, New Westminster (on the Fraser River a short distance to the southeast of Vancouver), and the provincial capital, Victoria, at the southern end of Vancouver Island.

The west coast of North America had been explored in the late 1700s by Captains Cook and Vancouver. Early in the 1800s, the westward expansion of the land-hungry population of the United States threatened British claims to the so-called Oregon Territory; in search of a secure base, British colonial officials and the Hudson's Bay Company founded Fort Victoria on Vancouver Island in 1843. A dozen years later, roving prospectors discovered gold in the untracked wilderness of the British Columbia interior, prompting a gold rush largely of Americans who came north from the worked-over gold-fields of California. To gain control of the British Columbia interior, the British established the city of New Westminster near the mouth of the Fraser River. Burrard Inlet, now the port for the City of Vancouver, was considered to be a potential route for a surprise attacker, but otherwise had little economic or strategic importance, as the Fraser River was the only practical route into the mountainous Interior and its rumoured Eldorado.

The gold rush more or less collapsed by the early 1860s, and several disillusioned goldseekers decided to try farming around Burrard Inlet and along the banks of the Fraser River downstream from New Westminster. A few entrepreneurs started sawmills along Burrard Inlet, and wrestled with the difficult terrain and monstrous trees; trade commenced with Van-

---

Above: *Vancouver's City Hall was completed in 1936 and was formally opened during the city's 50th birthday jubilee.*

Opposite: *The Hotel Vancouver, finally completed in 1939 after a seven year delay during the depression, was opened for the Royal visit of King George VI and Queen Elizabeth.*

5

couver Island, San Francisco, Australia, and even "around the Horn" to England. An innkeeper named John Deighton built a saloon on the waterfront just west of the Hastings Mill. Being something of a windbag, he earned the moniker "Gassy Jack," and before long the community of little hotels, bars, and shops which sprang up around Deighton House along today's Water Street to serve the workers at the nearby mill became known as Gastown, although it was officially christened Granville in 1870.

For the next dozen years, the denizens of little Gastown slumbered, drank, swatted flies and sawed the huge logs. Political types gravitated to New Westminster and Victoria, where they debated the issue of confederation with faraway Canada, and during the 1870s wrung their hands and threatened to secede over the issue of a transcontinental railway—the big promise which had convinced them to become Canadian (rather than remaining as English colonists, or joining the United States). After years of delays, a syndicate of capitalists in Montreal formed the Canadian Pacific Railway Company and, with generous public subsidies secured, set out to build a transcontinental railway line.

But where was the Pacific coast terminus to be? Victoria was the biggest city, carrying the most votes, and had received a federal government promise that it would be the terminal city, although no one had any practical suggestion about bridging the gulf which made Vancouver Island an island. The future Prince Rupert site to the north was several hundred miles closer to Japan and the trading potential of the Far East, but if the railway line went too far north, the southern part of the province would certainly be dominated by the rapacious Yankees. Eventually, the decision went to Burrard Inlet as the terminus—the railway was to come to the first tidewater, at the narrow, mountain-strangled easternmost finger of the inlet, where an aggressive little town called Port Moody sat. However, when the general manager of the Canadian Pacific Railway, William Cornelius Van Horne, visited Port Moody, he disliked its cramped site for railway yards and docks and the lack of opportunity for real estate development, and decided to look a few miles to the west at the area around Gastown. He reportedly had a wonderful time, although he lost heavily at a poker game, and found there to be enough room for a major city on the gentle slopes south of the inlet, and tremendous potential for commerce centred on the wide, deep harbour in the lee of the wooded peninsula which became Stanley Park. Lacking only a suitably grand name, sleepy Granville stood at the threshold of greatness; Van Horne, with one eye on the past and the other on the future, reportedly said: "I name thee Vancouver."

Thus, Vancouver was invented. It was technology (the railway) and foreign capital (at least, money from Eastern Canada) which changed it almost overnight from a drizzly frontier town to a thriving metropolis. The older centres of New Westminster and Victoria sank into comparative insignificance. In a wild splurge of speculation, new Vancouverites poured in from the east and the south; in a cacophony of hammering and sawing, they built a new town among the stumps and puddles of the old Granville townsite. The city incorporated itself in April, 1886, and promptly burned down a month later, razing its shacks and shanties. Scarcely pausing for the ground to cool, the new settlers passed fire and zoning bylaws, and built it up again. Guiding the development, dominating civic politics, and erecting some of the biggest buildings to spur further prestigious construction, was the Canadian Pacific Railway, which had received a grant of 6,000 acres of prime land—the centre of the modern city, stretching practically from downtown to the Fraser River—in return for bringing the railway to the Pacific coast.

The city grew quickly for a few years, then slumped, then boomed during the Klondike gold rush of 1898, and gradually the fine marble and stone commercial buildings and sprawling suburbs of wooden houses spread until the beginning of the First World War. By that time, about 100,000 people lived here, and Vancouver had become a city, with an opera house and theatres, a sophisticated streetcar and interurban electric train system, *Empress*-class ocean liners in the harbour, and a diversified economy dependent on transportation, logging, and fishing. Booms and busts in the resource industries, more war, and the Great Depression of the 1930s kept Vancouver more or less stagnant until late in the 1950s, when a rush of immigration and renewed prosperity in both the country and the world triggered the building boom which is still going on today.

Legacies of the past surround us. The distinctive Vancouver houses—wooden, shingled, with open porches and brackets in the eaves and picket fences—survive today in the ring of Edwardian-era suburbs around the downtown, including Strathcona, Grandview, Mount Pleasant, Kerrisdale and Kitsilano. Mature trees line the streets. A few of the oldest neighbourhoods, most notably the West End, the residential area between the commercial core and Stanley Park, have been redeveloped almost completely in the past thirty years with highrise apartments.

The Canadian Pacific Railway's effects on the city have been profound, and continue to be felt: the site of Expo '86 along False Creek, which is now being redeveloped in a luxurious fashion, was originally railway yards; Coal Harbour, the area of marinas and hotels along the waterfront between Stanley Park and downtown, is being redeveloped on other C.P.R. land; the city's SkyTrain rapid transit system snakes under downtown in a converted railway tunnel; the fine boulevards of Sixteenth Avenue and West King Edward Avenue were planted at the railway's behest; Shaughnessy Heights, the old residential area on the hillside south of the city centre, was planned and landscaped by the railway company; even the "centre" of downtown Vancouver, at the crossroads of Granville and Georgia, was determined by the railway company's manoeuvres of over a century ago.

Critics, with some justification, have described Vancouver as a setting in search of a city. Much of the development of the last two decades has softened their bite. An exceptional proliferation of restaurants, shops, and bars dots the downtown and adds a cosmopolitan touch to nearby residential areas. There are always new places to go, things to see and do. In the Kitsilano district, which was the hippie headquarters of western Canada during the sixties and seventies, there is still a counter-culture, but it coexists with a thriving, sophisticated over-the-counter culture in the shops and restaurants along Fourth Avenue. The city's old Chinatown, developed originally by laid-off railway navvies in the 1880s, continues to thrive in an enclave adjoining the restored Gastown. False Creek and Fairview Slopes, which were until recently an industrial backwater, now flourish with smart condominiums, easily the equal in their styles and sites and views of anything in San Francisco.

Vancouver is a city of long views, a city where you look over boulevard treetops and the shake roofs of wooden houses, or along streets which run down hillsides, to the towers of the downtown peninsula, encircled by water and framed by the snowcapped North Shore mountains. It is a city of flowering trees, beginning in January with the ornamental cherries on the boulevards and continuing through the fruit trees, horse chestnuts and dogwoods of April and May. It is a city of cottage gardens, and an almost endless English springtime from the snowdrops and primroses of January, to the camellias, daffodils and tulips of February and March, and the blazes of rhododendrons and azaleas in April and May. February is often gentle and quite balmy, the air soft, but March can be raw and blustery, sometimes including sudden snowstorms and quick frost which

Opposite: *The old Hastings Mill Store, one of Vancouver's first structures, and now a museum.*

smother the hardy early flowers.

There is a more rugged, classic west coast landscape along the shoreline of Burrard Inlet, around the university at Point Grey and on the steep banks above the picturesque coves of West Vancouver, where eagles nest in the windblown Douglas firs. The rainforest in these wild places is choked by thickets of salal and salmonberry; the seascape and rocky shoreline meet in a rolling canvas of greys and blues and cold, wet greens, with an occasional orange-barked arbutus tree, gnarled and twisted and swept by the westerlies, rooted tenaciously among the rocks. It is a craggy landscape with great plates of rock, the spaces between them full of moisture and an acid, fertile soil harbouring enormous thickets of spiky, thick-caned blackberries. Mint and lily of the valley spread like weeds.

Blue herons fish from tidal flats. Gulls wheel and cry. Fish boats bob, sails dot the harbour, clouds race. Layers of clouds, sometimes piling up in huge cumulus mountains, other times white and low and clinging to the trees along the seashore, interlock and unlock and blow up the valleys to the east. The sun sets over the gulf, framed by the distant Vancouver Island mountains, and colours the clouds with purple and orange, or catches the snow on the mountains and makes it glow like gold. In the summer, at twilight, there is an almost palpable hush over the city as the sun changes the vast ring of mountains to pink, then to purple, and finally to an infinite range of shades of indigo.

It is pointless to compare Vancouver with other cities. The city looks different, and feels different, from anywhere else. It is a west coast place, and the west coast of today has a distinctiveness all its own. The typical Vancouverite is fiercely proud and defensive of his city, rain and all. Throughout all this change, the "west coast style" is constant, and it is this conscious west coast identity that is defining the new Vancouver, and changing the old.

Above: *Vancouver's old courthouse has been refurbished and redesigned to house the Vancouver Art Gallery.*

Opposite: *Formerly the Expo Centre in 1986, the familiar landmark is now the Science Centre and houses four exhibition galleries, a theatre for scientific presentations, and the Omnimax Theatre.*

VANCOUVER
AND THE LOWER MAINLAND

The Inner City

The central core of Vancouver is made up of several neighbourhoods, each with its own distinctive character. The heart of the business district can be seen at a glance; its towers dominate the streets from False Creek to Burrard Inlet. To the east are the historic areas of Gastown and Chinatown. The West End a mixture of residential and commercial streets that has an ambience all its own roughly describes the area between Robson Street and Pacific Avenue, and between Burrard and Stanley Park. To the south and east of this downtown core spread largely residential districts that are loosely grouped into the East End and the West Side.

Historically, the nucleus of the downtown area was Gastown. Towering forests and isolated logging camps were all that was here when entrepreneur 'Gassy Jack' Deighton opened his pub in 1867, at the corner of present-day Water and Carrall streets. As Vancouver grew, the business centre moved away from Gastown and it began its decline into a rundown warehouse district. In the 1960s it was targeted for urban renewal and the Gastown of today was born: original buildings carefully renovated to house shops, restaurants, galleries, night clubs and warehouse residences, with cobble-stoned streets and wrought-iron lamp standards that recollect turn-of-the-century Vancouver.

To the south of Gastown is Chinatown, where crowds jostle along sidewalks lined with open-air produce stalls and the pungent smells of spicy foods emanate from dozens of bakeries and restaurants. Tiny storefront enterprises and large emporiums do a busy trade in items ranging from fine antiques to souvenirs costing just pennies. Chinatown has also been declared a historic area; its distinctive architecture, marked by Chinese influences in the rooflines and balconies, has been refurbished, and street signs and lamp standards have a Chinese motif.

The commercial centre of Vancouver's downtown district reflects the city's move into a period of radical new growth and an increasingly high international profile. The recent upsurge in well-designed multi-story buildings projects a new image and nowhere is that change more evident than at Canada Place an exciting harbourfront development completed in 1986. The facility houses the Vancouver Trade and Convention Centre, a World Trade Centre, the CN Imax Theatre, promenade shops, the elegant Prow Restaurant and Pan Pacific Hotel and a cruise ship terminal clearly inviting the international market to visit the newest player on the Pacific Rim.

Above: *Outdoor dining is popular during long summer days. This restaurant is Bridge's, located on Granville Island.*

Opposite: *Some of the city's office towers form a backdrop to Coal Harbour, and the many sailboats moored here.*

11

On a smaller scale are the chic shops, intimate elegant restaurants and casual eateries of Robson Street. The residential part of the West End has undergone a massive transformation since the 1950s when the 8-story Sylvia Hotel dominated the West End skyline. Now the area is one of the most dense in North America and 30-story buildings spike the skyline, interspersed with a few examples of Victorian wooden dwellings that have survived the upward expansion.

The West End is bordered along English Bay by a series of long sand beaches and a seawall walk. Across the water to the east is Granville Island, part of an innovative redevelopment scheme that blends private and public housing, retail development and public access to the waterfront with parks and an encircling seawall walk. To the far west are the lands adjoining the University of British Columbia, which occupies 990 acres (391 hectares) over-

looking Georgia Strait. Between and beyond, the residential areas Kitsilano, Shaughnessy, Fairview, Mount Pleasant, Dunbar, Marpole, Kerrisdale march south to the north arm of the Fraser River.

Above: *An aerial view of downtown Vancouver showing English Bay (bottom), Burrard Inlet (top left), and the inflated roof of B.C. Place Stadium (top right).*

Opposite: *Georgia Street, looking west towards Stanley Park, is one of Vancouver's main thoroughfares.*

12

Above: *The modern architecture of the new law courts located between Howe and Hornby streets. The building was designed by the renowned architect, Arthur Erikson.*

Opposite: *The B.C. Place Stadium with its teflon-coated roof. At the time of the official opening in 1982, the roof was the largest air supported structure in the world. The stadium has a seating capacity of 60,000.*

Previous Pages: *The Vancouver skyline from Coal Harbour.*

Above: *A member of the Vancouver Police force directs traffic at the corner of Hastings and Richards streets. The City of Vancouver boasts a police force of over 1,000 members.*

Opposite: *Shriners march down Hastings Street during the annual Pacific National Exhibition parade.*

18

Above: *The Vancouver Museum and Planetarium in Vanier Park occupies a site which was once a Musqueam Indian village. The area also includes the Vancouver Maritime Museum in nearby Hadden Park.*

Opposite: *George Norris' crab sculpture and fountain stands at the entrance to the H.R. MacMillan Planetarium.*

Above: *The Heywood Bandstand in Alexandra Park was built by the Vancouver Parks Board in 1914. It was restored in 1988 and is used today for outdoor concerts.*

Opposite: *The fountain in Lost Lagoon was built in 1936, and was a golden jubilee gift from the City of Vancouver.*

Previous pages, above and opposite: *Canada Place stands where the Canadian Pacific Railway's historic Pier B.C. was located. Construction of this multi-role facility started in 1983, and today Canada Place is home to a cruise ship terminal, the World Trade Centre, and the Vancouver Trade and Convention Centre. Also under its sails is the C.N. Imax Theatre, and above is the Pan Pacific Hotel with its nautical theme and fine restaurants.*

Above and opposite: *The Gastown area of Vancouver was named after "Gassy" Jack Deighton who opened up his famous Globe Saloon in 1867. The township of Granville grew up around his saloon, and eventually expanded into Vancouver.*
Today Gastown, with its cobblestone streets, is one of Vancouver's major tourist areas, and features pubs, restaurants, gift shops, and select offices.

Previous pages: *The city at night looking west from the Toronto Dominion Building at Georgia and Howe streets.*

Above and opposite: *The Pacific National Exhibition is held in the East end of Vancouver every year during the two weeks preceeding Labour Day.*
Attendance usually tops one million making the event one of the largest of its kind in North America.

33

Above: *The view from Granville Island across False Creek with the Aquabus crossing from the city.*

Opposite: *Granville Island marina from the Granville Street Bridge. In the background is the Burrard Street Bridge, the West End, and the North Shore mountains.*

Above: *An aerial view of False Creek showing the Burrard and Granville Bridges, and Granville Island in the center.*

Opposite: *The Granville Island Public Market is a popular shopping area where fresh local produce is available. The maket is open throughout the week.*

Following pages: *A crew from the Vancouver Rowing Club training in nearby Coal Harbour.*

The West Coast Transmission building (above left). The Lions Gate bridge (above right). Hastings Street looking west (bottom left). Robson Square and the Hotel Vancouver (bottom right).

Opposite: *Sailboat silhouetted at sunset in English Bay.*

Above and Opposite: *The Chinatown area of Vancouver is the second largest in North America and has had a colourful and varied history. The tenacity of the Asian culture is reflected in the distinctive architectural style of the area. A walk through Chinatown today will illustrate the recessed balconies, intricate woodworking, and ornamental wrought iron.*
Every year the community celebrates the Chinese New Year with a parade and other cultural displays such as the dancers above.

Above and opposite: *The Vancouver area boasts many beaches, but none are so popular as those around English Bay. In the summer months beaches like Kitsilano, Jericho, Locerno, and English Bay itself are always crowded.*

Previous pages: *Charter boats under the Burrard Street Bridge.*

Above: *The Museum of Anthropology at the University of British Columbia is based on traditional northwest coast Indian buildings. The museum houses a superb array of native artifacts and exhibits.*

Opposite: *The University of British Columbia the province's oldest and largest university was approved in principle in 1908. Today U.B.C. as it is known offers various degrees ranging from sciences, arts, and law, to medicine, education, forestry and commerce.*

Following pages: *Simon Fraser University sits atop Burnaby Mountain, and is another of the many fine buildings designed by Arthur Erikson.*

The North Shore

The overriding characteristic of the North Shore is the presence of the mountains. Lightened by the welcome sun, obscured by picturesque tendrils of fog, socked in by heavy rain clouds or brilliantly outlined by a dusting of snow, they reflect the constantly changing panorama of the seasons. They also provide the setting for a variety of recreational pursuits: skiing and hiking top the list.

The North Shore is the area to the north of Burrard Inlet, extending from Indian Arm in the east to Howe Sound in the west. At the foot of the mountains are the districts of North and West Vancouver, which encompass the larger cities of North and West Vancouver and smaller communities such as Deep Cove and Horseshoe Bay.

The first settlement in North Vancouver was established around a logging camp. The community continued to develop along industrial lines, and major railway and dock facilities for handling of grain and other commodities are prominent features of the city. As North Vancouver expands up the sides of the mountains, it also develops its amenities at the water's edge. Lonsdale Quay Market is at the North Vancouver terminus of the SeaBus, which links North Vancouver to the SkyTrain rapid transit system. The large, airy, skylighted structure at the Quay is a popular stop for commuters and a destination for visitors. It houses a produce market, retail fashion outlets, a variety of restaurants and a hotel on the top floors.

West Vancouver, linked by the Lions Gate Bridge to Vancouver, developed first as an exclusive enclave for wealthy Vancouverites. To this day it retains the feeling of a small, sleepy village with a somewhat British flavour: there are few highrises here, no heavy industry, and restaurants and retail stores are on a small, intimate scale. The shoreline, including Ambleside Park, which extends for 3/4 mile (1.2 km) along the seashore from the Capilano River bridge, offers wonderful views of Stanley Park, the Gulf of Georgia, and a variety of recreational, shipping and cruise boats as they navigate the turbulent tidal narrows under the Lions Gate Bridge.

The recreational areas on the North Shore are easily accessed in fact, most are within a half-hour drive of downtown Vancouver. The onset of winter is eagerly awaited by avid skiers, who can take their pick of several

Above: *The Capilano Suspension Bridge hangs 69 metres (230 feet) over the Capilano River and leaves many visitors breathless as they cross the canyon.*

Opposite: *The serene waterfront and harbour in Deep Cove.*

Previous pages: *The Lions Gate Bridge. Completed in 1938 it was then the first fixed link between Vancouver and the North Shore.*

venues. Winter sport facilities at Mount Seymour Provincial Park, Grouse Mountain and Cypress Bowl include downhill and cross-country runs, snowshoe trails and toboggan runs. On a clear day there are stupendous views of the city and surrounding areas, including the lower mainland, Georgia Strait and Mount Baker, in Washington. If the weather cooperates, the facilities are open at night, giving skiers the incomparable thrill of seeing the lights of the city spread far below as they negotiate the slopes.

During the summer, these areas are a popular destination for hikers and sightseers. An abundance of birds and wildflowers, vast forests and pristine mountain views can be enjoyed within minutes of civilization. Cypress and Grouse Mountain operate lifts during the summer months for sightseers and hikers.

For a true taste of the luxuriant coastal forest, Capilano

Canyon and Lynn Canyon Park are unsurpassed. The parks were created around Lynn Creek and the Capilano River, whose rushing waters have cut deep gorges in the rock. Suspension bridges over both rivers offer the thrill of swaying high above the river as mist rises from the swirling waters. Further west, at waterfront Lighthouse Park, large bluffs overlook the water and provide unrestricted views of Vancouver and Georgia Strait.

Above: *The Seabus, one of two catamaran ferries, crosses the Burrard Inlet every 15 minutes.*

Opposite: *The Lonsdale Quay Public market.*

Following pages: *The coast mountains at dawn from the Mount Seymour ski area.*

Above: *The Grouse Mountain Skyride operates year round transporting people to the top of Grouse Mountain 1,100 metres (3,700 feet) above the city. From the peak the panoramic view stretches from Vancouver Island to Mount Baker in nearby Washington State.*

Opposite: *The Royal Hudson passes through Dundarave in West Vancouver en route to its terminal in North Vancouver.*

Above: *The twin peaks of The Lions were originally known as the 'Chief's daughters' or 'The Sisters' according to local Indian legend.*

Opposite: *The British Columbia ferry terminal at Horseshoe Bay in West Vancouver. From here ferries sail to Vancouver Island, the Sunshine Coast, and other islands in Howe Sound.*

Above: *The grave of Chief Dan George can be seen at this Indian cemetery on Dollarton Highway near Deep Cove.*

Opposite: *St. Paul's Church on the Squamish Band Reservation in North Vancouver.*

Previous pages: *The Point Atkinson Lighthouse in Lighthouse Park, West Vancouver.*

Avove: *The view of Vancouver at night from the Vancouver lookout point in Mount Seymour Provincial Park. This popular area offers skiing, hiking, camping, horseback riding and other outdoor sports for visitors and residents alike.*

Opposite: *The Capilano River winds it's way down from the Cleveland Dam and enters the ocean near the Lions Gate Bridge. Each year salmon return to the Capilano River and swim upstream to the fish hatchery.*

Following pages: *Vancouver, and in the distance the mountains of Vancouver Island.*

Above: *The North Shore has many industrial areas along the waterfront. From this aerial view sulphur and wood chips are loaded for export to Pacific Rim destinations.*

Opposite: *Sunrise silhouettes the cranes of the Versatile Pacific shipyards.*

Parks and Gardens

Over 100 years ago, Vancouver city planners set aside a large chunk of land at the edge of a largely uninhabited, heavily wooded peninsula in reserve for a park. Today Stanley Park is a wooded oasis in the centre of a bustling metropolis, a luxury in terms of land size alone 1,000 acres (405 hectares) that no modern city could afford. But it is land well spent. Located within its boundaries are a wide array of facilities, from soccer pitches and baseball diamonds to peaceful trails through the forest, seaside swimming pools, two freshwater lakes, a world-class aquarium, two zoos and glorious formal gardens. It is a source of pride and pleasure to many thousands of residents who use the park regularly and is estimated to draw over two million visitors annually.

Perhaps that first park set the standard for Vancouver, and the mild climate certainly encourages the use of the outdoors and the establishment of parks. In any case, there are a number of very fine parks and gardens in Vancouver and environs, ranging from large wooded tracts with little development to display gardens and recreational parks.

Queen Elizabeth Park is a lovely example of the art of transforming quarry pits into beautiful gardens. In the early part of the century, stone was taken from Little Mountain to pave the city's first streets. Much of the hillside had been logged, and over the years the site became a popular spot for local residents to enjoy the far-ranging views. Land for the park was acquired in 1929, but it wasn't until the 1950s

that work was begun on the gardens. Today the 130-acre (53-hectare) park is a showpiece for the city. It boasts magnificent sunken gardens and broad grassy areas that allow sweeping views of the city from the park, at 500 feet (152 m) the highest point in the City of Vancouver. The triodetic dome of the Bloedel Conservatory, which houses 500 species of plants and 35 varieties of birds in a tropical environment, was completed in 1969.

VanDusen Botanical Gardens are a pleasure for any casual plant lover, and an education for the serious gardener. Thousands of species of plants are grown in a wide variety of theme gardens interspersed with peaceful lawns and water features. VanDusen Gardens have extensive collections of plants that do well in this climate, such as rhododendrons, hollies and hydrangeas. Because of their focus on experimenting with new plants, particularly those that come from similar climates, such as China, Japan and Korea, they have one of the most comprehensive collections of plants in Canada.

Above: *Springtime in the gardens in Stanley Park.*

Opposite: *This totem pole in Stanley Park is a symbol of the Coast Salish Indians.*

Nitobe Memorial Garden, located on the U.B.C. campus, encompasses two types of Japanese garden: a small formal tea garden (used on ceremonial occasions) and a larger *kaiyushiki*, or stroll, garden that reveals a different vista at every turn of the path. Established in 1960, Nitobe Garden honours a great humanitarian who worked for world peace, Dr. Inazo Nitobe. The garden offers a uniquely peaceful experience and an opportunity to enjoy the feeling of serenity evoked in a classical Japanese garden.

The outlying areas of Vancouver also have a fine array of public gardens. Fantasy Gardens in Richmond takes a playful approach to display gardening with their village and castle, but their two main gardens, the Biblical Garden and the Show Garden, display annual plantings at their best. Minter Gardens in Chilliwack, established in 1980 at a quarry site, integrates the natural west coast surroundings with a fanciful use of topiary. Park & Tilford Gardens, known for their lavish Christmas light displays, have been a North Vancouver landmark since their establishment in 1968.

Above: *A beluga whale at the Vancouver Aquarium. Belugas are widely distributed throughout the Arctic and are sometimes called 'sea canaries' due to their varied vocal repertoire.*

Opposite: *This 5.5 metre (16 feet) high statue of a killer whale stands near the entrance to the Vancouver Aquarium. The bronze sculpture was a gift to the aquarium and is the work of the eminent Canadian artist Bill Reid.*

Following pages: *The new whale pool at the Vancouver Aquarium is home to daily shows.*

Above and opposite: *Penguins and otters are some of the many animals in the Stanley Park Zoo.*

Following pages: *Built in 1913, the Stanley Park Pavilion was once the scene of elaborate dining and dancing. Nearby the Malkin Bowl offers outdoor theatre performances during the summer months.*

Above: *The seawall and Siwash Rock from Ferguson Point in Stanley Park.*

Opposite: *The Devonian Harbour Park with the Vancouver Rowing Club and Stanley Park in the background.*

Previous pages: *One of the many shady walks in Stanley Park*

Above: *The wooden bridge at the west end of Lost Lagoon in winter.*

Opposite: *Coal Harbour, Stanley Park, and the North Shore mountains in the background.*

The VanDusen Botanical Gardens on Oak Street encompass a 22.5 hectare (55 acre) landscape of plantings and quiet waterways. Located on the grounds is the MacMillan Bloedel Forestry Building, a facility which interprets the forests and forest industry of British Columbia through displays, films, and activities.

Above: *Each year thousands of lights herald the Christmas season.*

Opposite: *A heron stands silently by one of the lily ponds.*

Above: *Nitobe Garden, which is located on the campus at the University of British Columbia, is a blend of fir and cedar with classical Japanese arrangements of shrubbery, waterfall, bridges, and small trees.*

Opposite: *Dr. Sun Yat-Sen Garden is a part of the Chinese Cultural Centre. The garden was designed in China and is the only classical Chinese garden to be built outside China.*

Queen Elizabeth Park is on 'Little Mountain', the highest spot in the city. At the top are two abandoned quarries that have been transformed into huge sunken gardens.

Above the gardens is the Bloedel Conservatory; a plexiglass dome which houses tropical plants and flowers together with brightly coloured tropical birds.

Above: The Bloedel Conservatory

Opposite: The ornamental gardens in Queen Elizabeth Park.

Above: *Fall in Crescent Park in the exclusive residential area of Shaughnessey.*

Opposite: *One of the small lakes in Central Park in Burnaby. The park is also home to Swangard Stadium where local and international soccer games are held.*

Above: *The Carillon Bell Tower at Fantasy Garden World in Richmond. Each spring Fantasy Garden World features over 1,000 varieties of tulips, daffodils and other bulbs in a magnificent floral display covering 11 acres.*

Opposite: *The Minter Gardens are located near Chilliwack in the Fraser Valley. The gardens have extensive floral plantings during the spring, summer, and fall seasons.*

The Lower Mainland

The City of Vancouver is a relatively small core of 44 square miles (113 square km), but surrounding it are the municipalities that make up the metropolitan area; together they give Vancouver the third largest urban population in Canada close to 1.5 million. Many of these communities and bordering municipalities cluster along the Fraser River, once the main artery of transportation and communication for the region.

Just as the ocean has been an all-pervasive influence on the development of Vancouver, so the Fraser River has helped to mold the character of the city and its outlying areas. From its tumultuous mountain route through the Fraser Canyon it passes through Hope, where it begins the transition to the valley. As it travels westward it opens into a fertile delta, splitting into two main arms and forming many islands in its race to the sea.

Richmond occupies the two largest of these islands: Sea Island the site of Vancouver International Airport and Lulu Island. While today Richmond is increasingly becoming a residential and industrial community, it is based on rich farmland. Characterized by many small market farms it has been rightfully called the 'Berry Capital of North America'; summertime brings a feast of fresh produce to shoppers on its rural lanes. Fishing has also played an important role in Richmond's development. Steveston is a community of wide streets and old wooden buildings that recall the quiet fishing community of a century ago. But it is also one of B.C.'s busiest fishing centres today, and a large fish processing plant here is kept busy processing the catch from the commercial seiners and trawlers.

To the east of Vancouver are Burnaby and New Westminster. Burnaby is the home of Simon Fraser University, a mountaintop campus of striking modern design. Located on Burnaby Mountain, it affords magnificent views of Indian Arm far below and the mountains retreating to an impossibly distant horizon. New Westminster is today regaining some of the glory of former years, when it proudly claimed the title of 'Royal City'. Its waterfront development connected to downtown Vancouver via the SkyTrain rapid transit system is injecting this community with a new vigour. Restaurants and walkways allow a unique view of a working river, as fishboats, barges, tugs and log booms create a constantly changing vista on the wide sweep of the Fraser River.

Located on the broad plain south of the Fraser River are Delta, Surrey and Langley. The housing needs of the ever-expanding metropolis are devouring more and more of this

Above: *The Alex Fraser bridge is Vancouver's newest span over the Fraser River. At the time of its opening in 1986 it was the longest cable stayed bridge in the world.*

Opposite: *An early summer morning near Maple Ridge*

The Pattullo bridge in New Westminster (top left). The B.C. Tel building in Burnaby (top right). The International Peace Arch at White Rock (bottom left). Minoru Chapel in Richmond. (bottom right).

rich agricultural land, but residential areas are interspersed with wide fields dotted with grazing animals or neatly cultivated rows of produce. The area boasts a sunny climate with the mountains forming a much diminished backdrop far to the north.

Travelling east along the river, the mountains gradually grow closer and the population centres become less dense. To the north, the mountains close in more rapidly and the communities have settled between the deeply forested mountains and the river. In contrast to the broad valley, the mountains here are rugged and wild. Moisture-laden clouds blow in from the Pacific, creating a lush rainforest, and recreational areas have been carved out of the wilderness around rushing streams and clear glacial lakes. The south side of the river is characterized by an ordered, pastoral feeling. Picturesque farms and small communities Cloverdale, Abbotsford, Chilliwack, Rosedale are sepa-

rated by meandering roads that lead amongst neat, well-tended farms, peacefully grazing livestock, fields of grain and horse paddocks. Through it all runs the thread of the Fraser River, linking one community to another, past to present.

Above: *White Rock is the southwestern most community on the Canadian mainland and sits on the U.S.-Canada border.*

Above: *Fishing boats at Steveston at the mouth of the Fraser Valley. The old fishing village has a charm which comes from the past; its buildings of greying wood and wharfs lined with boats from a contrast to the modernized fishing industry which processes millions of pounds of fish each year.*

Opposite: *Log booms such as these can be found along the Fraser River from Hope to the estuary.*

Following pages: *Dawn on the Alouette River.*

Above: *Fishing at dawn in one of the numerous fishing holes in the Fraser Valley. This one is on the Pitt River.*

Opposite: *This farm lies in the shadow of Golden Ears Provincial Park. The Park is within easy reach of the city and is open all year. Among the variety of habitats here is lowland coastal forest, and large lakes such as Alouette, Pitt, and Stave Lakes.*

Above: *The Fraser Valley near Hope. The valley's rich soil is silt which the Fraser River has gathered on its journey from the Rocky Mountains.*

Opposite: *Fort Langley, a Hudson's Bay Company trading post was inaugurated in 1858. The original fort was completed in 1841, and today visitors can inspect the old buildings and learn about British Columbia history from several guides in period costume.*

Above: *The Benedictine monastery of Westminster Abbey overlooks the Fraser Valley at Mission City.*

PHOTO CREDITS: Michael E. Burch—Page 6, 9, 10, 13, 14, 16–17, 18, 19, 20, 23, 26, 27, 40, 44–45, 54, 58–59, 60, 63, 64–65, 66, 67, 68, 69, 70–71, 72, 78–79, 80, 86, 87, 95, 96, 97, 99, 102. **Larry Goldstein**—Pages 28–29. **Bob Herger**—Page 1, 12, 34, 35, 36, 37, 52–53, 55, 62, 74, 75, 76, 81, 88, 90, 98, 100, 103, 104, 106–107, 108, 109, 110, 111, 112. **Al Harvey**—Pages 82–83, 105. **J.A. Kraulis**—Page 4, 15, 32, 48, 50–51. **Rick Marotz**—Page 102. **Derik Murray**—Pages 38–39, 84–85. **Marin Petkov**—Page 5, 101, 102. **Michael Robertson**—Page 57. **Brian Stablyk**—Page 3, 8, 11, 21, 22, 24–25, 30, 31, 33, 41, 42, 43, 46, 47, 49, 56, 61, 73, 77, 89, 91, 92, 93, 94.